Introduction to Canning

Beginner's Guide to Safe Water Bath and Pressure Canning

Linda C. Johnson

© Copyright 2022 - All rights reserved.

The content contained within this book may not be reproduced, duplicated or transmitted without direct written permission from the author or the publisher.

Under no circumstances will any blame or legal responsibility be held against the publisher, or author, for any damages, reparation, or monetary loss due to the information contained within this book, either directly or indirectly.

Legal Notice:

This book is copyright protected. It is only for personal use. You cannot amend, distribute, sell, use, quote or paraphrase any part, or the content within this book, without the consent of the author or publisher.

Disclaimer Notice:

Please note the information contained within this document is for educational and entertainment purposes only. All effort has been executed to present accurate, up to date, reliable, complete information. No warranties of any kind are declared or implied. Readers acknowledge that the author is not engaged in the rendering of legal, financial, medical or professional advice. The content within this book has been derived from various sources. Please consult a licensed professional before attempting any techniques outlined in this book. By reading this document, the reader agrees that under no circumstances is the author responsible for any losses, direct or indirect, that are incurred as a result of the use of the information contained within this document, including, but not limited to, errors, omissions, or inaccuracies.

Table of Contents

Table of Contents	3
Introduction	7
Chapter 1: What's the Deal With Canning Food?	9
The Modern Significance	9
The Benefits	10
Hobby or a Lifestyle?	12
Chapter 1 Takeaway	13
Chapter 2: What Are You Going to Need?	14
Let's Talk About Canners	14
Other Supplies You'll Need	15
Why Location Matters	17
Chapter 2 Takeaway	19
Chapter 3: Introduction to Water Bath Canning	20
What Is It?	20
How Do You Do It?	20
Beginner Water Bath Canning Recipes	22
Is It for Me?	26
Chapter 3 Takeaway	27
Chapter 4: Introduction to Pressure Canning	28
So What's the Difference?	28
The Pressure Canning Process	28
Beginner Pressure Canning Recipes	30
Which Is Better?	37
Chapter 4 Takeaway	38

Chapter 5: Canning Safety	39
Common Mistakes	39
Introduction to Canning Meat	40
Is It Worth the Risk?	42
Chapter 5 Takeaway	44
Conclusion	45
Glossary	48
References	49
Image References	50

Your Free Gifts!

Out of all of the available literature on canning, you chose this one. Thank you. As a way to express my gratitude, I'm offering additional valuable resources for FREE to my readers.

Get Free Instant Access by clicking on or going to

www.customercore.eu

- **FREE GIFT:** My Ultimate Checklist For Canning Successfully
- **FREE GIFT:** My 5-Minute Cheat Sheet To Help You Can Safely
- **FREE GIFT:** My 17 Essential Items You Need To Can Successfully
- **FREE GIFT:** Is My Ultimate 35-Step Cheatsheet For Water Bath Canning Successfully every time
- **FREE GIFT:** Is My favorite (& secret) Pizza Tomato Sauce Recipe.

Before we start, I have a small favor to ask of you. When you finish reading this book, **would you please consider posting a review of this book on the platform?** Posting a review will help support my writing.

Thank you. I really appreciate it.

Just follow the relevant link below.

>> Click here to leave a review on Amazon and see my other books on Food Preservation <<

Introduction

The beginning is always today. —Mary Shelley

Welcome to the wonderful world of home canning. As someone who started their own canning journey many moons ago, I can assure you that this experience will not only be fulfilling but can actually be life-changing. I understand that this may sound cliché, but once you've finished your first batch of home-canned goods, you'll know exactly what I mean. There are a million reasons why you have decided that now is the right time to learn this new skill. Whether you want to start a business, be healthier, or just want a companion hobby to gardening, there's only one place to start: the beginning.

Beginnings are usually accompanied with feelings of excitement and fear. These two emotions will be your greatest assets. Without fear, we throw caution to the wind and that is when accidents happen that could easily have been avoided. Most mistakes don't matter in the long run, but unfortunately there are some deadly consequences. As for excitement, this emotion is a precursor to passion. Having a passion for what you are doing will be your greatest weapon in creating a journey that will lead to places beyond your initial expectations.

Developing your skills and knowledge will not be easy. There's a lot to learn when it comes to basic canning procedures. Canning isn't rocket science, but it is still a science. Processing times and method limitations aren't suggestions. Safety should be your utmost priority and the best way to do that is research, research, research. Your canning journey isn't a race; it's okay to take extra time to thoroughly understand something. As long as you're willing to put in the time, you'll have no problem mastering the craft.

Chapter 1: What's the Deal With Canning Food?

Examination of our past is never time-wasting. Reverberations from the past provide learning rubrics for living today. –Kilroy J. Oldster

The Modern Significance

To understand the modern significance of canning food, we first must understand its past. While food preservation has been around for thousands of years, the method of canning is relatively new. The journey began in 1795, in the ever-fashionable country of France. Their latest trend of the time, on par with their western counterparts, was revolutionary wars. The notorious French General Napoleon Bonaparte had realized that fighting on a battlefield was quite detrimental to one's nutritional health. To solve this issue, he offered 12,000 francs to anyone who could find a new way to preserve food. Fifteen years later, in 1810, a French chef named Nicolas François Appert would earn that reward when he introduced the world to canning.

Over the next 200 years, canning would make its way across the world, being improved upon every step of the way. While industrial canning has never gone out of style, home canning has often peaked in popularity during wartime or food shortages. The last large peak in the United States was in the 1930s and 1940s. Since this time, the United States has certainly faced its fair share of war and food shortages, so why haven't we seen the same increased levels of home canning? In truth, there's likely a million ways to answer this question but to keep it short and simple, we just want to be lazy now. The industrialization of food consumption has made the entire culture around home canning feel obsolete. Why grow and can your own food when you can pay for someone else to do it?

Here's a fun secret that consumerism doesn't want you to know: it's not sustainable. The amount of food waste caused by big-name grocery stores trying to create an atmosphere of abundance is catastrophic. Aisles are stocked full of produce that won't ever sell because there's too much of it. Instead of being donated to those in need, it spoils and contributes more waste to the ever-growing landfills. It's not just the stores at fault for this waste either. Food loss will occur at every step in the food production-and-supply chain. While loss is usually caused by spoilage, oftentimes food is thrown away just because it's ugly. One little blemish can cause a perfectly edible apple to get chucked in the bin. The planet is being destroyed, all for achieving an aesthetic.

Big corporations and consumerism culture will tell you that canning and home food preservation is a thing of the past—like dial-up internet and guillotines. In truth, it could be our last saving grace. We've spent the last 200 years perfecting this method. All the hard work is already done. Canners are incredibly safe; we know about, and how to prevent foodborne illness, and best of all there are a million delicious recipes to try. When it comes to the most prevalent issues we are facing in modern times, canning—as simple and historic as it seems—can play a significant role in preserving and protecting our planet. All we have to do is try.

The Benefits

There are numerous benefits to starting a canning journey, but let's start with the most brag-worthy. Canning helps the environment by limiting your food waste. According to the United States Environmental Protection Agency (EPA), ⅓ of all the food in the United States goes uneaten. The EPA also estimated that in 2018 American households contributed 20.3 tons of wasted food to the ever-growing landfills across our nation (U.S. Department of Agriculture, n.d.). Not only are the massive mountains of trash unsightly, but there are also pits of festering toxins that are slowly destroying our ozone layer. The most dangerous greenhouse gasses they emit are carbon dioxide and methane. Methane, in particular, is very dangerous and has already helped in the creation of a hole in the ozone layer located above Antarctica. Now if Antarctica was home to thousands of poisonous snakes I would say good riddance, but unfortunately it belongs to the most dapper of birds, the penguin. Every time you fire up that canner, you are effectively helping to stop the unhousing crisis in Antarctica.

Now let's talk about the benefits of canning on a less global scale. When you decide to can your own fresh ingredients, you are completely in charge of your health and nutritional wellness. Your family should know every ingredient that they are putting into their bodies. Half the time I can't even pronounce the ingredients I find listed on store-bought canned goods. For those who suffer from digestive issues or have specific diet restrictions, the canned aisle can be a minefield. Stop letting these big corporations with money signs for eyes, bully you into whatever is convenient. Your health should be in your hands and thanks to canning, it can be.

While we like to act all bashful and say it's not about the money, sometimes it's about the money. When you first start canning, the expenses will start piling up. The cost of equipment, utensils, and amazing resources like this one can become a little overwhelming. Just keep in mind that canning is an investment. As long as you stick to it, you can make way more money than you put in. Many people have a positive experience with selling their goods but by just successfully canning your first batch, you've already had a return on your investment. The point of canning is preservation. Americans waste thousands of dollars every year on food they never eat. That is just throwing money, nutritional value, and hard work down the drain.

While there are so many wonderful benefits to canning, I feel like one of the most underrated is feeling a sense of accomplishment. Participating in consumerism culture is easy but ultimately unsatisfying. Not only does your hard work pay off when you preserve, but you also have the option to be ethical. Whether you're growing your own food or supporting your local farmer's market, you know where the product is coming from. In a world where the priority is meeting the demand to supply as fast as possible, we can forget that the easy way can have serious repercussions. When we can, we can protect ourselves from participating in unethical activities of big corporations.

Hobby or a Lifestyle?

As a beginner, it's most likely you just want to eat your garden's strawberries in the wintertime. You're only planning to use your canner a couple times a year. Saving the world and having a strong sense of accomplishment sounds like a job for a superhero. That might be a multimillion-dollar film genre but it doesn't sound like a very fun or possible hobby. This fast-paced world keeps us busy and not everyone has the time to can every meal. Some days it's easier to just go to your local fast-food joint than to cook dinner. What's even the point of trying to learn this new skill if we can't maintain the lifestyle?

This begs the question, can canning just be a hobby or is it meant to be a lifestyle? At the end of the day, canning is just putting food in jars so you can eat it later. It does have great benefits but it's really not that deep. You shouldn't feel any pressure to be the perfect canner. I have never met an expert canner that hasn't at some point messed up and had to discard food. Accidents will happen and that's perfectly fine. The penguins are not relying solely on you to get your recipe perfect. One mistake is not going to undo all of your good intentions and hard work.

There isn't a debate about whether people who can as a lifestyle are better than those who can as a hobby. Your canning journey should not be dictated by what others may think of it. What matters is what you and your family need. This is what makes canning a journey. As you learn and improve, you will figure out what works with your schedule, diet, and personal tastes. If you decide to can less often once you find these reference points, that doesn't decide whether you're an expert or not. Just remember to always go with your gut feeling, pun intended.

Chapter 1 Takeaway

- Thanks to its 200-year-old history, canning has had a long time to evolve into the safe procedures we use today.
- Canning has numerous benefits including protecting the environment, being budget-friendly, and contributing to good health.
- No matter if you're canning as a hobby or a lifestyle choice, your journey should be unique to your own circumstance.

Chapter 2: What Are You Going to Need?

It's not about what equipment you have, it's what you do with it. –Aphex Twin

Let's Talk About Canners

Choosing your home canner will likely be the most important decision you'll make on your canning journey. While that may sound daunting, it should actually be a fun experience. Canning is meant to be personalized. You get to take the reins of your own kitchen and figure out what will work for you and your family. Canners come in a variety of sizes, types, and brands. Don't be intimidated; this is all for you to find the best fit for what you want to can. Keep in mind that the shiniest brand-new canner on the market isn't always the right choice. It's like buying a car but without the headache of a salesman.

Popular Brands

Presto and All American are two popular brands of Pressure Canner

Presto   All American

There are many things to consider when buying a canner. Most significant is whether you want a water bath canner or a pressure canner. This might sound like an exaggeration but the decision could literally mean life or death. Certain foods can only be canned in a pressure canner. Pressure canners reach higher levels of heat than their water bath counterparts. Without these high temperatures, harmful bacteria can spoil and poison your goods. Trust me, no one wants botulism for dinner. On the other side of the coin, some foods will lose their flavor and become overcooked if they are canned at higher temperatures. These types of food are not susceptible to botulism anyway. Pressure canning also takes longer which isn't ideal, considering canning is already a time-consuming activity.

Buying a canner may seem expensive but it's actually very accessible. Most retail stores that have an emphasis on kitchenware will have them, but the easiest and least expensive option is finding them online. On the high end, pressure canners can be upwards of $500. That, and the additional price of other supplies, would make this hobby unattainable for most families. Luckily, doing your part for the planet can be done on a budget. There are plenty of viable options for under $100. Canning can actually help you save money in the long run, so don't get tricked into thinking forking over the big bucks will get you the best results.

On average, water bath canners are going to be less expensive than pressure canners. They are essentially a large and deep pot with a rack and lid. As long as it can fit several jars on a rack with 1 inch of water covering them, any big pot will do. Pressure canners are a little more complicated when it comes to additional features. The lids are twist-on to keep them from flying off when the pressure rises. They also have dials, gaskets, and vents that make the process a little more complicated than water bath canning. If you are buying secondhand, make sure your pressure canner is from after the 1970s. Vintage is cool but not when it can blow a hole in your ceiling.

Other Supplies You'll Need

If you're going to be canning from home, you'll need glass mason jars. It may be tempting to reuse any commercial mayonnaise or sauce jars made of glass but this should be avoided. Jar breakage and seal failures are more common with these due to how they are manufactured. Mason jars are produced so they can withstand the canning process. With proper care and storage, you should be able to reuse your mason jars for years. They also come in a variety of sizes, so make sure to choose a size that will fit your canner and what you want to do. Wide-mouth jars are going to be easier to work with for beginners, compared to the regular mouth. You also might want to start off with smaller jars so less product is ruined in case you do make a mistake during your first trials.

Just because the jars will last you a long time doesn't mean the lids will. Most mason jars will come with a two-piece lid—the actual lid and the metal screw that keeps it in place. The lid piece will have a gasket around the edges that will ensure the seal. After one use, the gasket material will not seal properly and can become a breeding ground for bacteria. According to the National Center for Home Food Preservation, lids that are older than five years should be properly disposed of due to the gasket piece no longer being viable. The screw piece can be reused as long as there are no defects that could affect the sealing process.

The rack is where the jars will sit during the canning process. No matter if you're using a pressure canner or a water bath canner, you'll need a rack at the bottom of the pot. This helps with heat distribution. You will want all parts of the jar to be surrounded by the water. If the jars sit at the bottom of the pot, the food will heat unevenly and the contents in the bottom of the jar will burn or become tough and unsavory. The direct heat could also break the glass. While any rack will do, it will pay off to invest in one that will keep the jars from moving during the process. If the jars are constantly hitting each other, they can develop cracks that will cause bigger problems down the road.

As for things you'll want but aren't necessarily essential, jar lifters and funnels are definitely on the list. Jar lifters are utensils that are similar to tongs but are stronger. After the canning process is finished, you'll need a safe way to remove the jars without dropping them or burning yourself. Most modern kitchens are going to have funnels and ladles anyway but they are a great help for a faster food preparation. You'll want to save time without cutting corners in any place you can. Speaking of time, anything you can use like a kitchen timer or a phone alarm will help make sure nothing is overprocessed. Another utensil that will come in handy is a headspace tool that can get rid of bubbles before you seal the jars.

Why Location Matters

No matter what type of canner you're using, it's likely you'll be able to find thousands of different recipes. When you're first reading through them, you might notice the phrase "adjust to altitude" next to the processing instructions. This is because your location can directly affect your equipment and how to use it. Both water bath canners and pressure canners are affected by the altitude at which they are used. This is because both methods will require water to boil. At higher altitudes, water will boil at a lower temperature. If you are using the method of water bath canning, you have to extend the processing time to make up for this. For a pressure canner, you'll need to adjust the pressure.

While this beginner's guide and its companion books are packed full of information, not every one of your canning questions can be answered, especially when it comes to your specific altitude. Don't give up on your canning dreams just yet though. Your county will most likely have a local extension office you can contact about any questions you have regarding this. This is a great resource in general, especially if you plan on canning your own home-gardened produce. The U.S. Department of Agriculture (USDA) and the National Center for Home Food Preservation's websites also provide resources on finding your altitude. This might have better results than just a quick google search. Applying the wrong altitude adjustments could lead to unprocessed and inedible food, so you'll want to be as thorough as you can.

You should double-check with your local extension office but here are some basic guidelines for applying altitude adjustments. If you are using a water bath canner and are in a place with an altitude anywhere from 1,000 to 3,000 feet above sea level, you'll need to add five minutes to your processing time. With every additional 3,000 feet, add another five minutes. So, at 3,000 to 6,000 feet above sea level you'll add 10 minutes, then at 6,000 to 9,000 feet you'll add 15 minutes, and so on and so forth. For pressure canners, it depends on what type of gauge you're using. If you have a dial-gauge, you should add 1 pound of pressure per 2,000 feet. If you are using a weighted gauge, it's 1o pounds of pressure for anything lower than 1,000 feet and 15 pounds for anything higher.

The time doesn't just change for the actual canning process either. Cooking times can change too. If you're preparing food to be canned, it's a common occurrence to have to blanch it first. Blanching is a food preparation technique to help soften fruits, nuts, and vegetables where they are briefly immersed in hot water or hot oil. You should add a minute to your blanching time if you are in a place that is 5,000 feet or more above sea level. This also goes for other preparation steps such as sterilizing times for your jars. For every 1,000 feet above sea level, boil the jars for an additional minute.

Chapter 2 Takeaway

- There are two methods to canning preservation and they are water bath and pressure canning.
- Jars, and utensils such as a jar lifter, are an important part of the canning process.
- Altitude can affect the processing time and applied pressure of canners.

Chapter 3: Introduction to Water Bath Canning

Water bath canning is the simplest and most accessible of the two canning methods.

—Preserve and Pickle

What Is It?

A water bath canner is a large pot with a rack at the bottom for holding the jars. It will require a lid to cover the pot during the canning process. The rack is detachable so there is no specific difference between any large cooking pot and a water bath canner. As long as it can hold your jars with at least an inch or two of space above it for water, it should work. This makes the water bath canner the far more accessible choice when it comes to canning methods.

Water bath canners work by using boiling water to process the jars. This means that they can only reach the temperature of boiling water, which is 212 °F. This low temperature environment is most ideal for fruits, and foods with levels of high acidity. This is because the lower pH levels that cause the acidity can destroy harmful bacteria without the help of higher temperatures. Water bath canning these foods also stops them from becoming overcooked and has the best quality-based results.

How Do You Do It?

Before you can start putting your food in the jars, you must prepare them. Some recipes will call for sterilizing the jars first. This can be done by placing them—without the lids—in the water bath canner right side up and covering them with hot water. The jars should be fully submerged and there should be at least 1 inch of water above them. Bring this to a full rolling boil and let it stay boiling for 10 minutes. If your food requires less than 10 minutes of processing time, it is essential to sterilize your jars first.

Now you can start filling the jars. Make sure there are no air bubbles and wipe the rims before screwing on the lids and putting the jars back in the canner with a jar lifter. Wait till the water has reached a full rolling boil to begin timing the process. This is also when you should place the lid over the pot. Once the timer has run out, turn off the heat and let the jars sit for 10 minutes. When it's time to remove the jars, be careful not to take them out of the canner in a way that could disrupt the sealing process.

The jars should be left on a cooling rack for the next 12-24 hours. You will know your jars have properly sealed when you gently press down on the lids and they don't move or pop up. The screw bands will no longer be necessary and can be taken off and set aside to be used again. Store the canned goods in a dry and cool place like a dark pantry or basement. For the best quality, use within the first year of storage.

Beginner Water Bath Canning Recipes

To help you start your water bath canning journey, here are a few beginner friendly pressure canning recipes taken from my book "**Water Bath Canning for Beginners and Beyond!** The Essential Guide to Safe Water Bath Canning at Home. Easy and Delicious Recipes for Jams, Jellies, Salsas, Pickled Vegetables, and More!"

Straw-Berry Good Jam

Straw-Berry Good jam is a healthier alternative to sugar-packed store options. This jam uses honey instead of granulated sugar to sweeten, which infuses it with the honey's antioxidants and anti-inflammatory properties. Honey is also less processed than granulated sugar. The best time to prepare Straw-berry Good Jam is in June, when the berries are in peak season, depending on where you live: for example, strawberry season starts earlier in southern states.

Amount: Two 8 oz jars.

Ingredients:

- 1 ⅓ cups crushed strawberries
- ⅓ cup unsweetened fruit juice
- 1 ½ tablespoons No-Sugar Needed Pectin
- ⅓ cup honey

Directions:

1. Prepare all of the equipment. Wash the jars and sterilize them if necessary. Add water to the canner but wait to boil.
2. In a large saucepan, mix the strawberries and fruit juice at a low setting.
3. Then gradually add and stir in the Pectin to the mix.

4. After this, add the honey and raise the heat to high. Once it reaches a boil, maintain stirring for one minute before removing the pan from the heat source.

5. Funnel the hot jam into a heated jar leaving a ¼ inch of space before wiping the jar's rim and putting on the lid.

6. Using a jar lifter, gently place the jars in the canner, making sure there are 1-2 inches of water above them.

7. Bring the canner to a boil and let it process for 10 minutes. (Adjust time for altitude differences.)

8. After the time is up, turn off the heat and remove the canner's lid. Let it stand for five minutes before removal.

9. To remove the jars, use your jar lifter and let them cool for 24 hours before checking the seal.

10. Enjoy your Straw-Berry Good jam!

Orange You Glad Marmalade

With any orange-based recipe, we must ask ourselves the inevitable question: Florida or California. It all depends on what you are looking for. Florida oranges may have the sweeter taste, but California has a thicker peel. Interestingly, the oranges that are typically used in marmalade, Seville oranges, are not even mass produced in the United States. The most popular oranges are Navel and Valencia. It all comes down to preference, and most kinds of oranges will hold up. The best time to make this marmalade is from November to May, during peak harvest season.

Amount: Six half pint jars

Ingredients:

- 3 oranges

- 3 cups water
- ¼ cup of lemon juice
- 4 ¾ cups of granulated sugar
- 2 tablespoons of pectin

Directions:

1. Thinly slice the oranges with the skin on, cutting off the bottom and top stems. Cut the slices again into four pieces.
2. In a large stockpot, mix the lemon juice, oranges, and water, and bring to a boil before letting it simmer for one hour. Stir when needed.
3. Prepare all of the equipment. Wash the jars and sterilize them if necessary. Add water to the canner but wait to boil.
4. Once the peel is tender, mix in the pectin and bring the pot to a rolling boil again. Then stir in all of the sugar at once and return to a boil, this time for four minutes, before removing the pot from the heat source and skimming off any excess foam.
5. Funnel the marmalade into a heated jar leaving ⅛ inch of space before wiping the jar's rim and putting on the lid.
6. Using a jar lifter, gently place the jars in the canner, making sure there are 1-2 inches of water above them.
7. Bring the canner to a boil and let it process for 10 minutes. Adjust time for altitude differences.
8. After the time is up, turn off the heat and remove the canner's lid. Let it stand for five minutes before removal.
9. To remove the jars, use your jar lifter and let them cool for 24 hours before checking the seal.

10. Enjoy your Orange You Glad marmalade!

Peachy Keen Chutney

Peach chutneys are generally a more Western-style version of a traditional Indian dish. Despite the fact that the state of Georgia is nicknamed the "Peach State," California is the largest contributor of the fruit in the United States. Attaining fresh and local peaches for your chutney will be easy since more than 20 states commercially produce them. The peak harvest season for peaches is usually from May to September, but since the fruit is so widely grown in the U.S. it's available multiple times throughout the year.

Amount: Five half pint jars

Ingredients:

- 3 pounds of peaches
- 1 ¼ cups of light brown sugar
- 1 ½ cups of apple cider vinegar
- 1 cup of golden raisins
- 1 small lemon, seeded and finely chopped, including peel
- ¼ cup fresh ginger, finely chopped
- 1 medium onion, peeled and finely chopped
- 1 small hot chili pepper, finely chopped
- ½ teaspoon salt
- ¼ teaspoon ground allspice
- ¼ teaspoon freshly ground black pepper
- ¼ teaspoon ground coriander

Directions:

1. Blanch the peaches for easy skin removal and then chop them up into ½ inch chunks.

2. Prepare all of the equipment. Wash the jars and sterilize them if necessary. Add water to the canner but wait to boil.

3. In a large pot, combine all of the ingredients and cook over high heat until the peaches are soft.

4. If the chutney seems too liquidy, raise the heat to thicken it. Once you've reached an ideal texture remove the mixture from the heat source.

5. Funnel the chutney into a heated jar, leaving ½ inch of space. Wipe the jar's rim and put on the lid.

6. Using a jar lifter, gently place the jars in the canner, making sure there are 1-2 inches of water above them.

7. Bring the canner to a boil and let it process for 10 minutes. Adjust time for altitude differences.

8. After the time is up, turn off the heat and remove the canner's lid. Let it stand for five minutes before removal.

9. To remove the jars, use your jar lifter and let them cool for 24 hours before checking the seal.

10. Enjoy your Peachy Keen chutney!

Is It for Me?

It is my recommendation to start your journey by mastering the water bath canner. It is definitely the easiest method to canning preservation and will be the quickest way to develop your skills. I suggest hot packing your favorite fruit for a trial run. This way you won't be so distracted by any complicated recipes and can focus more heavily on getting used to your canner. From there you can work your way up to slightly more complicated things such as jams, jellies, and pie fillings.

This suggestion is educated but it's not universal. At the end of the day, it's up to you to decide where to start and what food you would like to begin canning. After all, we do live in a society that loves to multitask, so maybe the complicated pressure canner might appeal to you more. You should also only can things that you will want to eat. The point of canning is to preserve food but if you end up throwing it out, then the point is rather moot.

A lot of canning is just finding a balance between what you want and what you are capable of doing. You should push yourself but not to the extent where the experience is no longer a positive one. Water bath canning is fast and simple but if you don't connect with it, that's no big deal. No two persons' journeys will be the same. You should be deciding for yourself and for your family whether this method will be your go-to or not.

Chapter 3 Takeaway

- Water bath canners are used to process high-acid food such as fruit.
- Boiling jars at lower temperatures will result in sealed and processed high-acid foods.
- Water bath canning is a great place to start when you're just beginning your canning journey.

Chapter 4: Introduction to Pressure Canning

A yearly check up for your pressure canner keeps your equipment in shape.

–MSU Extension Services

So What's the Difference?

There are several differences between the pressure canner and the water bath canner, but let's start with how to achieve the higher temperatures required to process low-acid foods. Due to their high pH levels and their inability to destroy harmful bacteria on their own, low-acid foods such as vegetables or meat should be processed at a temperature that exceeds 240 °F. The heat in a pressure canner comes from the steam of the water rather than the boiling water itself. This steam is created from the pressurized atmosphere within the pot that is maintained through gauges and release vents.

There are two different types of pressure canners, one that uses a dial gauge and one that uses a weighted gauge to decipher the amount of pressure being applied in the pot. The dial gauge tends to be easier to use but a weighted gauge tends to be more accurate. Dial gauges are often featured on older canning models, so make sure to perform yearly checkups to keep your equipment in working condition. Another unique feature of the pressure canner is the lock-in lid that will stop any pressure from being released during processing. When the pressure inside does release, it will be safely expelled through a vent.

The Pressure Canning Process

When it comes to preparation, sterilizing the jars is not as necessary but you will want to heat them before filling them. When you fill the jars, make sure nothing is on the rim. Excess fat and starch are some of the most common reasons for a bad seal, and need to be wiped away. Use your headspace tool to get rid of any air bubbles before tightly sealing the jar. To prepare the actual canner, there should only be about 2-3 inches of water at the bottom. Unlike the water bath canner, the water should not be covering the jars.

Once your jars are in place, lock the lid. The next step is to vent the canner through the vent pipe for 10 minutes. After this, add the regulator to the vent pipe to plug it. If you have a weighted gauge, adjust the regulator as needed. The regulator will start to rock and the heat will need to be adjusted for a steady rattling sound. For dial gauges, the processing time starts when it reads 11 pounds. Once the processing time is over, turn off the heat but don't open the lid. You'll want to wait for your safety valve to drop down or your dial to read zero. Remove the regulator before unlatching the lid. Open away from yourself to avoid steam.

Just like the water bath canner, you'll want to wait 1o minutes to let the jars cool slightly before you take them out of the canner. The next few steps are also the same. Use a rack for the 12- to 24-hour cooling period and keep the jars out of drafty areas. Temperature fluctuations can ruin the sealing process, just as mishandling the jars so soon after processing can. Remember to label your hard work with a date and name before placing it in a cool and dry location.

Beginner Pressure Canning Recipes

To help you start your pressure canning journey, here are a few beginner friendly pressure canning recipes taken from my book "**The Essential Guide to Pressure Canning for Beginners!** All-In-One Cookbook with Safe, Easy, and Delicious Recipes for Meals in a Jar! Successfully Can Meat, Soup, Vegetables, and So Much More!"

Dried Beans

Makes: 7 pint jars (500 ml) or 14 ½ pint jars (250 ml)

Ingredients:

- 2 pounds (907 g) dried beans like pinto beans, black-eyed peas, black beans, peas, kidney beans, etc.
- Boiling water, as required
- ¼ teaspoon (1.4 g) salt per half pint jar or ½ teaspoon (2.8 g) salt per pint size jar (optional)

Directions:

1. To start off, pick the beans for any dirt, stones, discolored beans etc. Rinse the beans with fresh water and soak in a large pot of water. Soak them for at least 12 hours. Discard the soaked water.

2. If you do not want to soak the beans for 12 hours, there is another way you can do it: Place beans in a saucepan and cover with water. The water should be at least 2 to 3 inches over the beans. Place the saucepan over high heat and wait for it to start boiling. Let it boil for two minutes and turn off the heat. Let the beans soak in the hot water for an hour.

3. Transfer the beans into a large stock pot. Cover the beans with fresh water and place the stock pot over high heat. When water begins to boil, lower the heat slightly and cook for about 30 minutes or until the beans are tender.

4. Now the next thing to do is to arrange the pressure canner, canning lids and jars. You need seven 1 pint jars (500 ml) or fourteen ½ pint jars (250 ml).

5. Pour enough water into the pressure canner following the manufacturer's instructions such that it is about 3 inches (8 cm) in height from the bottom of the canner. Place the canner on your stovetop over low heat. Place the jars in the canner so that the jars remain warm. The temperature of the water in the canner should be maintained at 180°F (82°C). Place the lids in a small saucepan of water over low heat on another burner.

6. Boil a kettle of water. Lift the jars from the canner and place over the towel. Sprinkle salt in each jar if using.

7. Carefully ladle the beans into the jars along with the cooked liquid. Make sure the beans are equally distributed among the jars. If the beans are not covered in water, pour enough boiling water to cover the beans to get headspace of 1 inch (2.5 cm) and make sure to remove bubbles using a bubble removing tool. Reassess the headspace and pour more water if required.

8. Take a clean damp cloth and wipe the rim of the jars. Place the canning lid on each jar using the lid lifter. Place the canning ring on each jar and tighten it as suggested.

9. Place the jars in the canner and process the jars following the manufacturer's instruction manual at 10 psi (69 kPa). Set the timer for 75 minutes adjusting for altitude if required. Once the timer goes off, turn off the burner.

10. Once you are done with the processing, let the pressure release naturally before opening the canner and taking out the jars. Let the jars cool completely on your countertop for no less than 12 hours. Wipe the jars with a dry kitchen cloth or paper towel. Make sure to check for the seals. Use the beans within a year.

11. **Serving suggestion**: You can use these beans to serve with meat or add it into soups or salads. Warm them up before serving.

Lentils with Vegetables

Makes: 4 pint jars (500 ml)

Ingredients:

- 1 ½ pounds (680 g) dried lentils
- 1-2 fresh celery stalks
- Five cloves garlic
- One large onion
- A large handful chopped greens like kale, Swiss chard, green cabbage or any other greens of your choice
- Two basil leaves, minced
- ¼ teaspoon (14 g) dried oregano
- 3 cups (710 ml) low-fat, low-sodium organic beef broth
- ¼ teaspoon ground black pepper
- 1/8 teaspoon (0.4 g) red pepper flakes or to taste
- ½ tablespoon (7.2 g) salt

<u>Serving instructions per 1 pint jar (500 ml):</u>

1. Grated parmesan cheese to garnish
2. Salt and pepper to taste
3. Any seasoning to taste (optional)
4. Chopped parsley to garnish
5. Some cooked noodles or browned ground beef crumbles (optional)

6. Squeeze of lemon or lime juice (optional)

Directions:

1. Place lentils in a large pot and cover with enough water such that the water is about 2 to 3 inches over the lentils. Let the lentils soak overnight. If you are short of time and are not able to soak them overnight, then place the pot over high heat and wait for the water to start boiling. Once the water starts boiling, let the lentils cook for two minutes. Turn off the heat and let them soak for an hour.

2. The following morning (after soaking the lentils overnight), have your other ingredients ready. Finely chop the celery stalks, garlic, and onion. Check the greens for any wild plants and discard them. Rinse the greens well and discard the stems. Chop the leaves into smaller pieces if desired.

3. Now the next thing to do is to arrange the pressure canner, canning lids and jars. You need four 1 pint jars (500 ml).

4. Pour enough water into the pressure canner following the manufacturer's instructions such that it is about 3 inches (8 cm) in height from the bottom of the canner. Place the canner on your stovetop over low heat. Place the jars in the canner so that the jars remain warm. The temperature of the water in the canner should be maintained at 180°F (82°C). Place the lids in a small saucepan of water over low heat on another burner.

5. Now add celery, garlic, onion, greens, herbs, broth, salt, and spices into a stock pot and place the pot over high heat on your stovetop. When the mixture starts boiling, lower the heat and cook for 15 minutes. Turn off the heat.

6. Lift the jars from the canner with a jar lifting tongs and place over the towel. Place funnel over the rim of the jars and carefully add lentils and vegetables into the jars using the slotted spoon. Fill the

lentils up to 2/3 of the jars. Make sure the lentils and vegetables are equally distributed among the jars.

7. Now pour the hot stock into the jars until you get a headspace of 1 inch (2.5 cm). If the stock is not sufficient, boil some hot water in a kettle and pour into the jars. Make sure to remove bubbles using a bubble removing tool. Reassess the headspace and pour more boiling water or hot stock if required.

8. Take a clean damp cloth and wipe the rim of the jars. Place the canning lid on each jar using the lid lifter. Place the canning ring on each jar and tighten it as suggested.

9. Place the jars in the canner and process the jars following the manufacturer's instruction manual at 10 psi (69 kPa). Set the timer for 75 minutes adjusting for altitude if required. Once the timer goes off, turn off the burner.

10. Once you are done with the processing, let the pressure release naturally before opening the canner and taking out the jars. Let the jars cool completely on your countertop for no less than 12 hours. Wipe the jars with a dry kitchen cloth or paper towel. Make sure to check for the seals. Use the lentils within a year.

11. **Serving suggestion**: Empty the contents of a jar into a saucepan. Heat the lentils over medium heat on your stovetop. Add cooked noodles or beef if desired. Add salt and pepper to taste. If you like to dilute the lentils, add some water or stock while heating the lentils. Ladle into bowls. Garnish with parsley and parmesan cheese and serve.

Baked Beans

Makes: 6 pint jars (500 ml)

Ingredients:

- 2.2 pounds (1 kg) dried navy beans

- 12 ounces (340 g) tomato paste
- 3 teaspoons (15 g) mustard powder
- 3 teaspoons (15 g) ground black pepper
- 2 tablespoons (30 g) kitchen bouquet (optional)
- 6 cups (1.5 L) cooked bean water
- Two medium onions, chopped
- 3 tablespoons (30 g) Worcestershire sauce
- 3 teaspoons (15 g) salt
- 6 tablespoons (90 g) brown sugar
- Four bay leaves

<u>Serving instructions per 1 pint jar (500 ml):</u>

- Sweet chili sauce to taste
- Chopped cooked sausages
- Salad or cooked pasta

Directions:

1. Place beans in a stock pot and cover with water. The water should be at least 2 to 3 inches (5 to 7.5 cm) over the beans. Place the pot over high heat and wait for it to start boiling. Let it boil for two minutes and turn off the heat. Let the beans soak in the hot water for an hour. Make sure to cover the pot while the beans are soaking.

2. Meanwhile combine onions, Worcestershire sauce, salt, brown sugar, tomato paste, mustard, pepper, and kitchen bouquet in a large microwave safe bowl. Keep it aside as of now.

3. Drain off the water and put the beans in a large pot. Add bay leaves and cover with water. The water should be at least 2 to 3

inches (5 to 7.5 cm) over the beans. Place the pot over high heat and wait for it to start boiling. Let it boil for 1-2 minutes and turn off the heat. Do not boil the beans longer than two minutes or else you will end up with mashed beans.

4. You also need to arrange the pressure canner, canning lids and jars. You need six 1 pint jars (500 ml). Pour enough water into the pressure canner following the manufacturer's instructions such that it is about 3 inches (8 centimeters) in height from the bottom of the canner. Place the canner on your stovetop over low heat. Place the jars in the canner so that the jars remain warm. The temperature of the water in the canner should be maintained at 180°F (82°C). Place the lids in a small saucepan of water over low heat on another burner.

5. Now place a colander over a large bowl and drain the beans into the colander. Do not discard the cooked liquid. You need some of it to make the sauce. The bay leaves are no longer needed.

6. Pour 6 cups (1.5 L) of the drained liquid into the microwave safe bowl with the sauce ingredients and stir. Cover the bowl and place it in the microwave. Cook on high power for about seven minutes. Or until you get a nice sauce. Take out the bowl and stir the sauce.

7. Distribute the beans among the jars. You should be able to fill each jar up to about ¾ the jar. Pour the sauce mixture into the jars until you get a headspace of 1 inch (2.5 cm). It is better to use a funnel while pouring sauce into the jars.

8. Make sure to remove bubbles using a bubble removing tool. Reassess the headspace and add more of the mixture into the jar.

9. Take a clean damp cloth and wipe the rim of the jars. Place the canning lid on each jar using the lid lifter. Place the canning ring on each jar and tighten it as suggested.

10. Place the jars in the canner and process the jars following the manufacturer's instruction manual at 10 psi (69 kPa). Set the timer for 65 minutes adjusting for altitude if required. Once the timer goes off, turn off the burner.

11. Once you are done with the processing, let the pressure release naturally before opening the canner and taking out the jars. Let the jars cool completely on your countertop for no less than 12 hours. Wipe the jars with a dry kitchen cloth or paper towel. Make sure to check for the seals. These jars will last you for 12 to 15 months.

12. **Serving suggestion**: There are numerous ways of serving baked beans. You can serve it over toasted bread. You can serve eggs over beans. You can serve it as a side dish along with meat. You can mash up the beans and serve as a bean mash. You can also make muffins or frittatas using the baked beans.

    Here is one favorite way I use the baked beans: Empty the contents of a baked beans can into a saucepan. Add sweet chili sauce and sausages and heat it over medium heat until very nice and hot. Serve it over hot cooked pasta or along with a salad.

Which Is Better?

To imply that there is a canning method hierarchy would be spreading false information. The difference between the two methods is not solely preferential. There are many variables to take into consideration, most of which are beyond our control. That isn't to say people don't develop their own biases on the subject, but the choice of which method to use is ultimately decided by the food you process. Unless we want to endanger ourselves, the only power we have in our choice comes from our ability to change the circumstances. To put it simply, the question isn't which is better, but rather which is better for what you want to do.

With all that in mind, the water bath canner is better. I am by no means omnipotent but I am willing to bet that you are reading this beginner's guide because you're a beginner. As stated in the previous chapter, water bath canners are oftentimes faster, easier to use, and overall, less time-consuming to master. Most recipes for water bath canners are beginner-friendly as well. You're less likely to make mistakes due to inexperience. As one of my dearest readers, I want you to have a safe and positive first experience canning home goods.

Pressure canning will be the better option once you have the experience and skill to tackle its unique features. There are so many more options for meals once you learn pressure canning. If you intend to can as a lifestyle, this skill is absolutely essential. You will need the protein and other important nutritional value found in low-acid foods for a healthy and well-rounded diet. While I do hope you take my suggestions into consideration, if you want to learn pressure canning first, it's not the end of the world. That only comes when we're irresponsible with our food waste. There's no set journey to canning but as long as you're passionate with a healthy sense of caution you'll be a success.

Chapter 4 Takeaway

- Pressure canners are physically different from water bath canners and reach higher temperatures.
- Pressure canners use steam to process and seal jars with low-acid food in them.
- There is no superior method, as both pressure canners and water bath canners are important for food safety.

Chapter 5: Canning Safety

Smart people learn from their mistakes. But the real sharp ones learn from the mistakes of others. –Brandon Mull

Common Mistakes

Most canning mistakes are not world-shattering as long as you know how to take care of them. One common conundrum for beginners is realizing that you've lost quite a bit of liquid in the jars after processing them. This could be caused by a number of things and doesn't necessarily mean the jar isn't sealed properly. Check the lid 24 hours after processing. It should be concave—if not, it's likely unsealed. Loss of liquid can be caused by not getting rid of the air bubbles before placing the jar in the canner. Another reason may be that the pressure was fluctuating too much during the processing. Another simple explanation is that the starchy food absorbed it all. No matter what the reason, don't open the jar to add more liquid or else you'll ruin the seal.

Another common mistake is when the jars don't seal properly. If you realize this within a few hours, you can try processing it again; otherwise, you should discard it. This may have been caused by a problem with the lid's gasket, or the jar could have a crack in its rim that went unnoticed. It could have happened when you took the jars out of the canner as well. They are still very vulnerable to unsealing during this time so make sure to be careful with the lids. Always make sure to double-check your equipment before you use it, to prevent any mistakes. You should also remember to wipe the mouth of the jar clean before putting on the lids. Any amount of residue can affect the seal.

Let's talk about signs of spoilage. If you notice a jar that has been on the shelf for a while starts to change color, there could be an issue. There are some products that just naturally turn different colors, such as apples and peaches. However, if the color is unsavory and you notice a distinct smell, throw it out. It's possible something went wrong with the processing or maybe an ingredient caused it to turn rancid. To prevent this in your produce, make sure you are canning it at the proper maturity level. Other signs of spoilage could be the liquid becoming cloudy, or finding sediment in your jars. This could also just be caused by the starch in vegetables.

One of the biggest mistakes new canners make is forgetting to clean your equipment. For most people, canning is seasonal. This means there's a large portion of time during which your equipment isn't being used. To prevent any unwanted rot or mold, your equipment should be thoroughly cleaned and dried before it heads to storage. Nothing will ruin a season faster than a giant rust stain on the side of your water bath canner. Canners and jars are made to last for years but they won't make it very long if they aren't properly cared for. It's also important to wash your equipment before you use it, to get rid of any dust or other strange residue that can clog vents.

Introduction to Canning Meat

When it comes to foods I'd recommend to beginner canners, meat is probably last on my list. It isn't necessarily harder to can meat than fruits, but there's more risk involved. If you are going to can any type of meat, you will need to use a pressure canner. Fish, poultry, pork, or any other kind of meat you can think of requires higher temperatures for safe processing. Water bath canners cannot reach these temperatures and will not kill off the dangerous bacteria. In case any of our vegetarian friends are wondering, meat substitutes such as soy or plant-based products don't necessarily follow these same rules and should be researched separately.

So why does meat require a pressure canner? Meat and poultry are low-acid foods which means their pH levels are 4.6 or above. Fruits and jams have high acidity and have lower pH levels. This is why they are safely processed in a water bath canner. Knowing the levels of acidity in your food is important because it will decide what type of canner you will be using. The rule of thumb is usually meats and veggies are low-acid, while fruits and their by-products are high-acid. This isn't always the case however. If you are unsure, don't make a guess based on taste. Look it up or ask your local extension service as they can help with any agricultural questions.

Clostridium botulinum is the most dangerous threat you will face on your canning journey. This is the spore-forming bacterium that causes botulism. Thankfully it can be annihilated by two things: high temperatures and acidity. Fruits and other high-acid foods are naturally protected because of their pH's inhospitality. Unfortunately, low-acid food pretty much has a welcome mat laid out for this dangerous foe. This is where pressure canners come in to save the day and satisfy our protein levels.

Just one taste of the botulism toxin can be fatal. According to the Centers for Disease Control and Prevention (CDC) website, the most common symptoms of foodborne botulism are vomiting, nausea, stomach pain, and diarrhea. If you have any reason to believe you've contracted botulism, seek medical attention immediately. This toxin works by attacking your nerves and causing breathing problems and paralysis. Even after the proper medical attention, the recovery time can be rather slow if the toxin has progressed enough. While only five out of 100 patients with botulism succumb to the illness (Centers for Disease Control and Prevention, 2022), it's better to be safe than sorry.

While you should be wary about botulism, don't let the very idea of it scare you away from canning meat. Your biggest worry should be about the type of meat you are canning. You'll want to use high-quality, fresh cuts. Any excess fat should be cut off and discarded. Heat can't penetrate fat as easily, so not only will the meat be undercooked but it will also be at risk for bacteria. Meat can be hot packed or raw packed depending on how you plan on eating it. If you choose to raw pack it, don't add water or broth like you would when hot packing it.

Is It Worth the Risk?

It is understandable to be cautious about canning after the last two sections. Don't worry yourself sick though. There are no huge risks to canning—except, of course, an uncomfortable and painful death by food poisoning; that, and having your pressure canner explode, blasting glass and burning hot food all over the place. Okay I lied, there are a few big risks to canning. Luckily, they are all easy to avoid. Canning has been around for over 200 years, which means that any mistake that can happen has already happened. There's a lot of information on the subject that can keep you and your family safe. In this modern age, the worst-case scenario is the least likely to happen.

Back in the 1930s and 1940s, canning was a lifestyle for the majority of American households. They did not have the resources or the fancy ultrasafe pressure canners of today. All they had was a little bit of food and a whole lot of gusto. While canning still has its risk today, it's nothing compared to back then. Due to food shortages, if they made even one little mistake, they'd be goners, but somehow they made it through one of the most difficult times in American history. Our great grandparents were pretty hard-core. If they can safely prepare dinner while fighting the Nazis, we can definitely do it using our high-tech appliances.

You are not alone. Keep in mind you are far from the first person to start their canning journey. Thanks to the internet, there is a whole community of canners, waiting to help you at any time. Whether you want to know how to spice your peaches or are just uncertain about what brand of jars to use, someone somewhere out there has an answer for you. There are so many amazing books on the subject, some of which are written by yours truly; and if there's one thing I know about canning, it's how to keep people from making avoidable mistakes.

So, to answer the question, is canning worth the risk? Yes, 100%. The risk factor is substantially low considering the likelihood of failure. The best tool for safety is knowledge and now that you know the risks and how to prevent them, that likelihood is nearly nonexistent. Did I mention that canning helps decrease the levels of CO_2 and methane in the atmosphere? These chemicals in large quantities are incredibly dangerous to life as we know it. What's worse: the very low possibility of contracting botulism or the very real possibility of destroying the entire planet? Considering everything, it's more dangerous to not use your canner.

Chapter 5 Takeaway

- Mistakes are common when you first start off but as long as you know how to handle the situation there will be no long-term issues.

- Meat and other low-acid foods are susceptible to botulism if not properly canned.

- As long as you take safety precautions, there is very little risk to canning.

Conclusion

The end is just the beginning. –T.S. Eliot

Before we finish this last leg of the race, I want to congratulate you on making it to the end. With everything you have just learned, you are now ready to start your first batch and begin creating your own personalized pantry. Thanks to canning's rich history, it can be one of the most beneficial experiences. In all of the excitement, don't forget to have all your equipment cleaned and ready to go. If you are using a water bath canner, make sure you are only processing high-acid food. If you prefer to start with the pressure canner, get acquainted with all its unique features to avoid mistakes. If you do make a mistake, take a deep breath and react accordingly.

While I tried to apply as much information as I could in this short guide, there's still a lot I've missed. If you want to learn more about canning or are looking for some great new recipes to try, take a look at my full-length books on the subject:

Pressure Canning Without the Danger! Your Comprehensive Guide to Safely Using Your Pressure Canner. With Tips, Tricks, and USDA Guidelines to Help You Use Your Pressure Canner Without Risks!

The Essential Guide to Pressure Canning for Beginners! All-In-One Cookbook with Safe, Easy, and Delicious Recipes for Meals in a Jar! Successfully Can Meat, Soup, Vegetables, and So Much More!

Water Bath Canning for Beginners and Beyond! The Essential Guide to Safe Water Bath Canning at Home. Easy and Delicious Recipes for Jams, Jellies, Salsas, Pickled Vegetables, and More!

Canning Mastery! 3-Books-In-One Compilation!

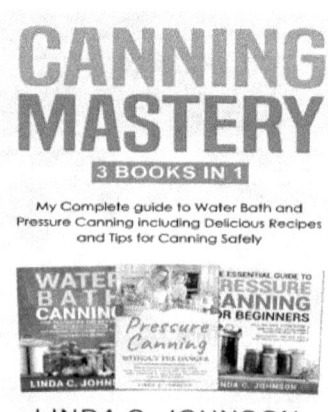

Thank You

Dear reader, I would like to take this time to appreciate you. Without your purchase and interest, I wouldn't be able to keep writing helpful books like this one. Once again, THANK YOU for reading this book. I hope you enjoyed it as much as I enjoyed writing it.

Before you go, I have a small favor to ask of you. **Would you please consider posting a review of this book on the platform? Posting a review will help support my writing.**

Your feedback is very important and will help me continue to provide more informative literature in the future. I look forward to hearing from you. Just follow this relevant link below.

>> Click here to leave a review on Amazon and see my other books on Food Preservation <<

Glossary

Botulism: A potentially fatal food poisoning caused by processing low-acid foods at temperatures below 240 °F.

Dial gauge: A dial that observes the pressure of a canner.

Food waste: Food that is not eaten and ends up in landfills.

Food Preservation: The process of slowing the rate of spoilage by treating and handling food.

Greenhouse gas: Potentially dangerous gasses caused by pollution that can have a detrimental effect on the environment.

Home canning: A method of food preservation where produce is sealed in airtight jars.

Nicolas François Appert: The French chef who is credited with the development of canning as a means of food preservation.

Ozone layer: A region in the stratosphere that protects Earth from the sun's rays.

Pressure canner: A method of canning where pressurized steam is used to seal and safely process low-acid foods.

Vent pipe: A part of a pressure canner that emits steam, allowing excess pressure to be released.

Water bath canner: A method of canning where boiling water is used to seal and safely process high-acid foods.

Weighted gauge: A weight used to control the pressure of a canner.

References

Alfaro, D. (2020, April 8). *What is blanching? It's a helpful technique to know.* The Spruce Eats. https://www.thespruceeats.com/blanch-480604

AZQuotes. (n.d.) *Aphex Twin quotes.* https://www.azquotes.com/quote/1488675

BrainyQuote. (n.d.). *T. S. Eliot quotes.* https://www.brainyquote.com/quotes/t_s_eliot_101421

Centers for Disease Control and Prevention. (2022, June 8). *Botulism.* https://www.cdc.gov/botulism/index.html

Chihak, S. (2022, June 20). How to use a pressure canner to preserve your veggies, meat, and more. *Better Homes & Gardens.* https://www.bhg.com/recipes/how-to/preserving-canning/pressure-canning-basics/

City of Alliance, Ohio. (n.d.). *The benefits of home canning.* www.cityofalliance.com. https://www.cityofalliance.com/322/The-benefits-of-home-canning

Clemson Cooperative Extension. (n.d.). *Canning meats & poultry.* www.clemson.edu. https://www.clemson.edu/extension/food/canning/canning-tips/51canning-meats-poultry.html

Fifield, K. (2016, December 14). *Testing your pressure canner.* Michigan State University Extension. https://www.canr.msu.edu/news/testing_your_pressure_canner

Healthy Canning. (n.d.). *Fat and oil in home canning.* https://www.healthycanning.com/fat-and-oil-in-home-canning/

International Food Additives Council. (2021, February 12). *From Appert to the Ball brothers: A history of canning.* https://www.foodingredientfacts.org/apperttotheballbrothers/

Moranville, W. (2022, August 16). Necessary canning adjustments for high altitudes. *Better Homes & Gardens.* https://www.bhg.com/recipes/how-to/preserving-canning/altitude-adjustments/

NASA. (n.d.). *Is the ozone hole causing climate change?* Global Climate Change: Vital Signs of the Planet. https://climate.nasa.gov/faq/15/is-the-ozone-hole-causing-climate-change/

National Center for Home Food Preservation. (n.d.). *How do I...can?* https://nchfp.uga.edu/how/can_home.html#gsc.tab=0

Oldster, K. J. (2015). *Dead Toad Scrolls*. BookLocker. https://booklocker.com/books/8700.html

Preserve & Pickle. (2019, July 11). *Water bath canning vs pressure canning*. https://preserveandpickle.com/water-bath-canning-vs-pressure-canning/

Shelley, M. (2014). *The Short Stories of Mary Shelley: Vol 2*. Miniature Masterpieces.

Unisan. (2022, February 9). *What is a landfill? Why are landfills bad for the environment?* https://www.unisanuk.com/what-is-a-landfill-why-are-landfills-bad-for-the-environme

U.S. Department of Agriculture. (n.d.). *Food waste FAQs*. https://www.usda.gov/foodwaste/faqs

Image References

Conti, F. (2018, June 28). *Mountain range view under blue sky during daytime* [Image]. Unsplash. https://unsplash.com/photos/BFFgACu5UXI

Daniels, K. (2019, June 10). *Clear glass bottle on white table* [Image]. Unsplash. https://unsplash.com/photos/BArWcH78kQ0

Graphic Node. (2019, April 5). *People standing near patio umbrella surrounded by fruits and vegetables* [Image]. Unsplash. https://unsplash.com/photos/N-AC7tTcD-c

Odintsov, R. (2021, January 18). *Woman putting homemade jam from the pot into a jar* [Image]. Pexels. https://www.pexels.com/photo/woman-putting-homemade-jam-from-the-pot-into-a-j

PublicDomainPictures. (2012, February 17). *Harvest canning preserves* [Image]. Pixabay. https://pixabay.com/photos/harvest-canning-preserves-14417/

Sigmund. (2021, February 1). *Three clear glass jars on blue and white textile* [Image]. Unsplash. https://unsplash.com/photos/WENdZ6LH9Pg

Theodore, J. (2019, July 4). *Clear mason ball glass jars* [Image]. Unsplash. https://unsplash.com/photos/gVIEmHgFRac

Tindell, M. (2020, February 22). *Man in black shirt sitting beside brown wooden table* [Image]. Unsplash. https://unsplash.com/photos/cz8fBPnt6VI

Tursunov, B. (2022, January 11). *Pollution concept, burning garbage pile in trash dump or landfill* [Image]. Unsplash. https://unsplash.com/photos/GmqezLxud8g

Yousaf, U. (2020, September 15). *Cutting and chopping meat on a wooden chop board* [Image]. Unsplash. https://unsplash.com/photos/r91GaM9be1s

www.ingramcontent.com/pod-product-compliance
Lightning Source LLC
Chambersburg PA
CBHW050209130526
44590CB00043B/3359